MY TALK – BOOK THREE
THE RISE OF MICHELLE JEAN

In life we fall but it is up to us to pick up self and rise again. Yes there are many pitfalls but after the pitfalls are over, you can only go up; move up to a better and brighter life; way.

Yes I've fallen but it's now my time to rise and shine with you. The tears were there, I felt the pain and hurt; lived in sorrow. Now I am ready to put all that behind me and rise, rise again. I must be progressive; move forward and gain; gain all that is positive, prosperous and true in my life from God – Good God and Allelujah, Earth and the Universe.

Michelle Jean

I am no longer a prisoner, I am free, free to be me and be with you. My life has been hard, filled with a lot of pitfalls and sorrow but all that is done now. I am free; released. I did for you Good God and you did do for me and I truly thank you, but now I have to rise, rise up to you in glory for me and you.

It's March 31, 2015 and the mood is different; free from my shackles and chains; lifetime of hurt and pain.

I am no longer bound to death.
I am no longer bound to him.
No longer bound by her.

I've completed one leg of my journey with you Allelujah hence I release all my anger, pain and hurt when it comes to you because I am free. **Now I am listening to Mr. Vegas, RISE AGAIN on this day.**

Like he said, **"it's going to take time to get over you."** But I am not letting you go Good God, I am letting go of the things and people that truly hurt me. I need to live, hence I have to let go of my children and tomorrow will be the first step in letting all that hurt me with them including them go.

Yes I will fall because I will not have a place to go but this is okay. I am happy with this. I am released Good God, I am released. Yes I know it will take time for me to rise but this is okay. Some of my hurt and pain will be gone.

I will no longer have to sacrifice my health to feed them. I won't have to push for them (my children) to get up and go to school to achieve something that will benefit them in the long run.

My eldest finished college and I am truly proud of him. Yes he's going to go back to school hence I will do all to help him once I rise. He deserves it more than all because I know the truth and good heart I have in him and he has for me. He's faced the challenge and challenges with me and it's now up to me to ensure he has a blessed and secure future financially as well as with you.

My second, child I will make provision for him because despite it all, he is there for me in his way. My desire for him is that he goes to college and achieve something good for him. He also trusts you Good God, so truly secure him and yes I wholeheartedly take away the 1/10th of one percent that I commissioned for him. He is deserving of more hence I am giving him more.

Yes my life is at peace since I've kicked out my last one. The stress and anger is no longer there. Hence my daughter is next to go. Well the rest of them will be going soon, hence I must rise health wise because a lot of my stress will be gone.

Yes it will be hard for me not seeing them on a regular basis but I cannot sacrifice anymore of me for them.

I cannot slowly kill myself because of them.

I have to live because my life has been shortened. So whatever time I have left on this earth, I have to dedicate it to your good service in goodness and in truth Good God and Allelujah.

I have to continue to dedicate myself to you and for you because you deserve all my goodness as well.

You are a great friend and keep hence I am keeping you.

Hey, hold your head up because I truly thank you for all you've done for me. This is our new beginning and I am truly glad I am beginning with you.

You are my heart and soul; true and good spirit, so truly be proud of you. You did well by me and you.

You are my good thought and thoughts, hence I know true love. I also know that anyone that want and need true love can find it. True love is attainable and that true love is you.

<u>**Yes you are my rise and fall, but on this day you are my rise; upright eye in triangle.**</u>

You are more than my hope; you are my true and wonderful friend.

You are my gorgeous mother and father.

You are my good and unconditional all. So truly be proud of you and all that you do. No other god can do what you do. You created it all and gave to man, but man did not want your true all, hence they've let you go and accepted someone else.

Worry not yourself because I do accept you. So take my hand and feel me; feel the goodness I have in me for you.

Smile and truly love you.

Lovey we will rise because you are my sea and seas; good water and waters of life. Hence shortly, I will be on the sea with you and we will dance and be free like a dancer in motion; expression.

You are my world and universe and one day I will build you a better, richer, newer, fuller, prettier, purer, cleaner, honest and whole world and universe for me and you. So rise with me in a good and true way my Lord and God, rise with me.

Come on Lovey take my hand and rise with me. We are together and I share all with you equally and more than equally because you were truly there with me in my storm and storms of ills and pain; sufferings.

You and I can never be over hence you are my time, timeline, healer and true friend; all.

Yes humanity may not be with you, but I am with you holding your hand, blasting you, encouraging you, truly loving you and being truly honest with you.

Lovey we can't let go of each other and I truly don't want or need to. Yes there are many ills and pain in this world, but as humans we are the ones that need to change self and let go of the hurt and pain we feel as well as let go of all the hurt and pain that come our way.

As humans we cannot continue to hold on to things that hurt us and I've learnt this. Yes I am afraid of hurting people's feelings to the point where I hurt myself and live in this hurtful pain and I can no longer do this.

Good God and Allelujah, I've told you you've hurt me, but in my hurt and pain you needed something of me. You needed me to shut out and shut down all facets of wickedness and evil more than infinitely and indefinitely forever ever without end and I hope and pray that I've done this with you and for you.

Lovey, I truly don't want to hurt you and this is why I've told you I've made you my beating stick. I had to Lovey I had to because I do not know of a better way. I am letting go Lovey, I am letting go; letting go of all the hurt and pain in my life and world. Yes my children are important to me but I have to let go of their pain and hurt. I have to truly be me and in doing so, I will not let anyone tell me this or that about them (my children). I have to come to you Good God because you know the ordeal we went through. You alone can tell me what to do as well as teach them and you're teaching them, well some but the rest have to learn to listen and do better for self. Lovey, remember how I got sick and who had to stand up and be father and mother for the household so no shirt or skirt is going to tell me nothing.

Wow my true friend, if only all of humanity could truly learn to rely on you like I have.

If only humanity can feel my true and more than unconditional love of you while reading these books.

If only humanity can trust you like I do.

Ah Lovey I know my children have and has hurt me, but by me letting go I don't have to hurt anymore like I've said. As a parent that truly loves their children, there is only so much you can take.

Lovey look at Eve (Evening) and you.

Did you not let her go because she blatantly and willingly let you go for him?

Did not my son let me go and disrespected me with her?

So yes there comes a point in time as a parent you have to let go despite your hurt and pain. You cannot continue to live in hurt and pain.

You cannot continue to die because of wicked and evil children and people.

As a parent you can only take so much and I am truly not willing to die an early or spiritual death because of my children or anyone. I know the road you want and need me to take and I am taking it. I have to take it because you want and need to open good doors for me. I know I cannot attain and achieve you

living in a dirty environment, hence I have to make me and my surroundings clean and whole not just for me but for you also.

You want to come in and be with me and I have to let you in. I can't keep closing the door to you, this is not right. Plus I can't keep complaining to you. I need help, so I have to help myself in the interim.

Like you, when our children, spouse, anyone causes us pain we have to let them go.

<u>**No one can rise in hurt and pain**</u> come on now. When you are in pain you are stressed, can't think right and you think all sort of negative things and I cannot and or no longer live in or on the negative pathway.

Yes I am free from her and she concerns me not. I have to live because you held on to my life and secured me with you. Hence I have to journey on with you.

Yes pain and stress came.
Financial pain and stress came and is still there.
Health stress and pain came and is still there.

But with all this said Good God, if I was to die today, who would bury me?

Where will I be buried?

I've told you I do not want to be buried amongst wicked and evil people; hence I need you to secure my life. I need you to bury me once my spirit sheds the flesh if it does.

I know my spirit does not have to shed the flesh but whatever you decide in goodness and in truth, truly let it be because I truly need it to be so.

I need to be with you yes and this is my official step to meeting you and being with you.

Lovey, it's not all that want to learn the easy way. Many want to learn the hard way and when they get beatings they ask why like me. So yes I am truly happy that I am going to walk away from all that hurt me; cause me pain.

Yes I've done up my termination letter to the land lord and I am giving it in today Good God, and now reality has hit my second son. He is talking to you, taking his pain to you. He is angry but there is nothing I can do. I cannot continue on with them knowing my pain and health situation. They are grown children and they have to stand their own. I am not hurt I am leaving them on this day because I know they need to stand their own ground. I talk too much and now I cannot talk anymore. I've had to push and push and I cannot push anymore because they knew this day would eventually come. They now have to learn to fend for self because when I was telling them to go to school, get their college education they would not listen.

<u>My second child the one that is talking to you now said to me yet again, mom when I was a child I did not listen to you, I did my own thing. So what is the point of securing a place for children that do not listen? Now he's seeing things when it's too late.</u>

I've told my children to work and save their money, I will take the blunt force of it all and I have. But if a child do not truly listen how can I continue to take the blunt force of it all?

I am killing me emotionally, financially and health wise and I can no longer do this to secure children that truly do not listen.

Yes it's going to be hard on them but when I WAS GIVING THEM THE EASY WAY THEY DID NOT WANT IT. THEY REFUSED IT, SO HAVE THINGS THE HARD AND HARSH WAY.

I FACED HELL WITH THEM AND IN ALL I'VE DONE SINCE YOU TAKING ME OUT OF HELL WAS TO PREPARE A BETTER PLACE FOR THEM (MY CHILDREN) BUT THEY COULD NOT SEE THIS. I cannot take it anymore nor can I go on, move forward in pain.

I will no longer stay on the battlefield of death with my children because I am literally dying and I cannot lose my life because of them.

I cannot walk on the road of nastiness and shame with them.

I can no longer hold my head down in shame because of them.

It's like my niece told me, due to the situation she is going through, if you are not paying my rent I don't have to listen to you. She's facing hell but yet refuse to let go the person that is causing her pain. So because I am not paying her rent she does not have to listen and she must stay in pain and learn the harsh and hard way.

Lovey I have to let her be. Like I said, I have you but I cannot continue to let you walk away from me because of my children and the situation that I am in. Something has to give and I am giving. Yes I am prepared for my children to hate me because of this but it has to be. I have to go.

I have to get my health in check.
I need to live and enjoy my life with you.
I have to be made whole and clean.

My spirit needs this.

My soul need this and my body – physical body need this because it's in decay; ruin. I have to mend it and mend me and I cannot be soft because children don't know how to cope and or don't know what to do.

Like you GOOD GOD YOU I GAVE THEM THE EASY WAY. YOU GAVE HUMANITY THE EASY WAY AND WE ARE THE ONES TO CHOOSE THE HARD WAY. So yes I am letting my children be. YES I AM GOING TO LOSE IT ALL BUT SO BE IT. I'VE TOLD YOU I AM PREPARED TO FALL. I AM PREPARED TO LIVE IN THE STREETS.

I am mentally prepared Good God, Lovey I am mentally prepared and I will not blame you for this because this is the way it was meant to be. And somehow I know you will not let me end up in the streets. I know you will prepare a place for me.

Lovey I am broken all around and it's you that I have to lean on. I have to lean on you because you're all I have.

Right now my father's health is deteriorating and my brother is calling me to bury the hatchet with him but my spirit is not willing to do this. I cannot concede with him because every child is deserving of a father. You were there for me through it all and it is you that I have to look to and help.

You do not have children and grand children and abandon them, come on now.

You have great grandchildren and you don't know them. Come on what kind of nonsense is this, and now that you are up there in age and feeling the blunt of this you are saying we don't come around you.

Tell me something, as a grandfather what have my children learnt from you apart from abandonment?

What positive advice have you given them?

How many times have you told them happy birthday?

How many times have you called them to say Merry Christmas, happy birthday, how are you?

Absolutely none, so how can they (any of my children) look to you and say, granddad thank you for all you've done for me?

Good God it's hard, so hard and you know this. You know how I feel about truth and honesty.

How can I say to my children go help granddad if they know not him?

See we don't think of our future; getting old.

We don't think that when our children are hurt, feel hurt and abandoned that they remember this.

We don't think if we don't have anything to do with our children when they are young that they won't want to have anything to do with you when they are older and many don't.

Good God you cannot blame us for this.

You were there for me Good God, so why can't I be there for you?

Why should I be there for someone else?
Was it not you and my mother that were in the storm and storms with me?

So why should I abandon you both?

Children are important Lovey and if you don't save them when they are living, how can they save you when you are dead?

No come on think about it.

Did you and my mother not do all to save me from the dead and living?

So why would I not want to save you and her. Yes my father did some good to me, but the hurt and pain I felt due to him and his scum bag girlfriend outweighs any good he's ever done for me.

I know the angle of death.
I know what death tried to do to me but you never gave up on me.

Yes there are people in worse situation than me and in many ways you do spoil me. I am a spoilt brat at times when it comes to you I know this, but hey this is me and it's okay by me if you spoil me. Who wouldn't truly love you spoiling them?

Lovey none of us have to feel pain and hurt, but yet some of us cannot let go.

I can't change you; you have to want and need better for self and do better for self; change you. Yes a lot of us are weak and dying but you are there for them. Look how many times I am weak and can't go and you somehow give me that little bit of energy to go.

We all can change for the better if we want and need to.

We all can leave our abusive situation if we truly want and need to.

There is nothing that we can't do for self as long as it is good. None of us are determined by our environment.
No, that's not right; man's environment trap us hence we become mentally enslaved, conditioned and controlled. Therefore I cannot live in the society and societies of man because I more than desire freedom and truth.

Like I said, as humans you gave us the easy way but we are the ones to choose the hard way.

We are the ones to choose wrong and when death and or the wrong road beat up on us, we run and complain to you, halla anna ball bout life haade. Life isn't hard, our circumstances and or situations and environment we live in is hard. People make things hard for some of us. Our government make things hard for some of us. (Corruption and political affiliations)

A wi choose di hard road. And yes I know some of us are born on the wrong road hence we live on the wrong road.

But the man.

But the man what?

Did Good God not show you him in black descending down upon you? Eeee mean sey nuh choose him. He's your death angel. I learnt this the hard way.

But, but nothing. Good God gave you a song, it clicked in your head by informing you that he she was a cheater and not to get with him, and you are the one that did not listen. You ran down the road and or avenue with him her anyway, and now that your body is riddled with all manner of diseases and pain you are complaining to Good God whilst telling him he's not fair. <u>HE DID WARN YOU BUT YOU REFUSED TO LISTEN. YOU DID NOT ACCEPT HIS ADVICE; TRUTH.</u>

No, don't because your mama told you not to buy that dress because it did not fit you; it looked ugly and or inappropriate on you and now that your friends and foes are laughing at you, you are crying and saying you hate them. Your mother told you not to but yet you disobeyed. Stop because she told you not to buy those gaudy looking shoes but because they are in style you bought them anyway. Now you are out of pocket for more than $200.00. $200.00 that you could have used to pay down your phone bill and buy groceries. Now you are turning trouble to every and everyone including family. Need I go on come on?

You have your natural hair an coop pan di billions the black community spend on fake hair. Yes you included. Good God gave you natural hair that is filled with so much energy and some a unnu sey unnu nuh like eee, eee nasty.

Please, so a unnu nuh want good things. So stop complaining if you can't buy food and or formula for your children because you spent your hard earned money on fake and unnatural hair. Unnu waane wear haase batty, so don't complain when other nationalities call unnu ediat; foolish and dumb.

<u>No, don't because some a unnu skin bleachers truly need to take a look in the mirror and see how ugly and disgusting you all look. HENCE EVERY NATION AND OR EVERYONE GLOBALLY KNOWS WHAT THE WALKING DEAD LOOKS LIKE. YES UNNU LOOK LIKE DAMN DUPPY. WAIT SOME DUPPY PRETTIER DAN SOME A UNNU. Self hate is a sin hence many black people hate self. Would rather look like death and talk like death in the living.</u> Good God gave you beautiful skin and you're telling him unnu nuh want it. So when you are riddled with skin cancer and all manner of ailments, don't go to the hospital for free medical aid. Trust me if I was a government official, I would give you none because you willingly and knowingly choose self hate; to kill yourself. You bought these diseased products, so look to who you bought these products from for help. My medical system do not under any

circumstances promote self hate. Go someplace else with your nastiness and regressive cursed mentality.

So now tell me, if you choose all of this, why should Good God turn around and look at any of you; try to save you?

Yes my son is panicking right now because the simple life will not be there. He's going to have to pay rent and be on his own but this is okay. I tried and during my trying, I was disrespected and taken advantage of. And like I said, I have to live, I need to live because my life is worth it and I refuse to let any child kill me because they refuse to listen as well as leave everything on me.

I never set out to hurt any of them. I've always tried to secure a place for all of them and it's them (my children not all but some that did not want or need this; good for self. So yes reality has set in where we will all be homeless real soon.

I have no one's home to run to; hence where I lay my head now is where I will call home. I no longer have to put up with the slackness and nastiness you all bring to me and or into my home. If you all wanted goodness for self you would have secured goodness.

No family, I am getting bent. You are trying with your children and they are failing you and self. No they are failing self.

Don't tell God – Good God black kids are wicked. YOU JUST CHOOSE NOT TO LISTEN.

Many of you choose not to listen. When mama an daddy a talk, unnu sey dem foolish an nuh ha sense. Well now live on your own and accomplish the life you want and need to live for self. And don't talk about doing wrong things either. Mama and daddy and in many cases Mama alone and Granny alone a try an unnu mek it haade fi dem. Unnu a get goodness and instead of clinging to goodness and truth, some a unnu walk the folly ground and cause unnu loved ones heartache and pain. Look at your life. Think because **ALL THE EVILS AND OR BAD THAT YOU DO TODAY, AFFECT YOUR TOMORROW; FUTURE.** Some a unnu complain that you cannot get jobs after being in jail, but think, truly think, you've done all your wrongs, hurt people, killed people, so why now should someone turn around and hire you? You hurt others, caused severe pain and now you are expecting someone to give you a helping hand. Your mother and father counselled you for your own good and look at the shame and pain you have caused them, so why should someone turn around and give you a second chance? No I am not being harsh; I am getting you to think. **<u>Yes we all can turn our lives around, but why go through all that</u>**

when all the heartache and pain you were causing was not necessary. And don't give me my parents don't love me bullshit because it's not every parent know how to truly love. The love they know is the love they show you.

And forget it with daddy not being there. Mama is still there trying with you.

Granny is there trying with you.

Your aunt is there trying with you, so truly don't give me any excuses. **_A parent and or friend and or anyone that truly loves you will always be there for you even in death._** My mother truly loved me; I learnt that after she died, hence I've told you I have to save her and Good God. True love is not ungrateful hence I am different in every which way come on now.

My mother and grandmother raised me and I thank God – Good God and Allelujah for the truth and goodness they instilled in me. You are no different, so change you, do not let it get too late come on now.

Well I want my mother to love me.

Do you have a roof over your head?
Do you have food to eat?
Do you have clothes to wear?
Do you have shoes on your feet?

Is Mama not working two, sometimes three jobs to feed, clothe and shelter you?

Yes right. Now tell me, what are you doing that is positive for her? She's providing for you the best way she can, but you cannot see this because all you see is you; your selfish and greedy needs. Yes I know some of you are not this way, but a lot of you are.

Do you wash the dishes?

No right.

You don't even do your own laundry.
You don't cook or help to clean up the house.

Nothing you do to help her in a positive way, so how the hell can you say Mama doesn't love you? You don't truly love your mother because she's doing all for you and all you are doing is causing her heartache and pain. Come on now. **<u>True love is not one sided, love is, hence love is hate in my book. We all hate each other because we cannot love each other true.</u>** And I refuse to take this back Arnold, Joe and Frank including Robert. **<u>True love cannot hurt, love does hence it's not everyone that can truly love.</u>** If you truly loved your mother and or parents you would do to help her; them. Wash the dishes, do the laundry, start dinner if you are home before them (your parents), do your homework, get up in time to go to school, get good grades by going to class, hand in your assignments on time and stop letting your teacher call home to say you did not hand in your assignment and you did this and this to disrupt the class. There is so much you can do to help her (your parent or parents) but you don't. Instead you contribute to their heartache and pain.

Look at how many of you that are teenagers and pregnant. Tell me, can a child take care of a child?

You are pregnant and you expect Mama, the one you did not listen to to help you. Wow. Raising a child is not easy hence some of you are teenage mothers and feeling it right now.

He wanted a child and you had to give it to him. Well where is he?

Where is your education? Yes cut short for now.

Learn from life and others if you can. Meaning if you see someone struggling do not want to struggle like them. Stay home go to school and get your education. Your parents and or parent is giving you the easy road, take the easy road and leave the hard one alone.

Why add stress to your live if you don't have to. Mama say; wash the dishes it's your duty. Wash the dishes and not make her shout at you. Then yu sey shi miserable. You caused her misery come on now. Do what you need to do so that she does not have to complain come on now. Do your homework and your chores come on now. As parents we fuss and quarrel when you do not do what you are supposed to. If you do what you are supposed to then your parent (s) will not have a need to complain. If she or he complains then something is wrong with them come on now.

But my friends. Shut it. Your friends did not bring you into this world your parents did. And anyone who tells you to go against your parent or parents is not a good friend. Respect goes a far way so respect them (your parent or parents).

I know Joan you are going through hell because you are abused. You have an opening. There are places you can go and get help, get the help that you need because no parent has the right to beat you until you are black and blue. No parent have a right to sexually abuse you. No one has. This is bleeping wrong on your parents and or these people's part. Bun dem come on now. You are not his mate or wife you are his child and he should respect you as a child; daughter. Yes your mother should too and by her condoning his nasty and sick behaviour, she is as guilty as him and she will have hell to pay. She's not protecting you, she's killing you. You are her child and not because she's been hurt as a child gives her a right to hurt you. Suffering and pain was there yes, but over time you can get over and will get over. Behind the Scars for me is my testament and a tat of what I endured. I cannot edit this book nor look at it because it tells a lot of my hurt and pain. I can't even finish it. But despite it all, I am me. I am rising above my hurt and pain. I raised my children despite the hardships I face with them. They (my children) faced the hardships with me but there comes a time when you have to put the hurt and pain down and begin to heal. You have to heal. You may not be able to forgive them, but it does not mean you cannot live true and love true. Come on now. So hug me because I am hugging you. Yes I am squeezing you and drying your tears whilst moving your blonde hair from your face. Smile for me because I am smiling with you. I am there for you so truly take my hand and heal. Heal with me because we are on this journey together. I refuse to leave you and I refuse to lose you. So take my hand because there is that much trust between me and you. We can talk.

Don't because it's michellejeanbooks@gmail.com.

No buts use it. And please everyone let Joan reach me. Do not inundate my email with junk emails lest I get angry and ya'll know how angry I can be. I truly don't joke. Let her reach me because she needs me.

I know it's not Joan alone that needs me, you need me too. You have my email, email me.

Onwards I Go
There are no jobs. Well create one for you.

But, but nothing, create a job for yourself; you.

I'm a lawyer and I can't find a job, start your own law firm. You have a computer, make flyers for yourself and hang them up in laundry mats, grocery stores. Go to the mall and hand them out. Use your Facebook account to advertise for you if you can.

<u>Listen we all grow up and in growing, we have to make life choices not death choices.</u> You cannot live to hurt and kill, you have to live good and clean. Come on now. Secure your future because the life you save might just be your own.

<u>Like I said, Good God gave us all the easy way, we are the ones to choose pain and heartache.</u>

Did Eve (Evening) not do the same thing and she felt pain all around?

Did she not die all around?

So why are we carrying on with the death trend?

You want better listen to the good counsel of Good God come on now.

Good God never told you not to listen to good and true counsel, you chose not to listen. You choose to do your own thing and I cannot push anymore lest I fall down hard and die and this I cannot allow for myself.

I have to move on with my life no matter how difficult it will become.

Yes I more than over stand your concerns when it comes to my health but I have to do this. I have to make myself whole.

I have to do all by myself to get my health back on track.

I need to enjoy my life now.

I cannot let my children or anyone kill me.

NO CHILD CAN FAULT OR WRONG A GOOD PARENT FOR WANTING AND DOING GOOD FOR THEM; ABSOLUTELY NONE.

As children, learn to listen to good counsel. Yes some parents are wicked and evil but these parents I leave to hell because they know better but yet they carry on with the evil trend.

I refuse to be like them hence I've made my choice to stay with good, true, honest, clean and positive life always.

Many of you have it good but yet throw it away and when it's too late unnu run come bout mama, mama mi sarry. Unnu noa di truth but refuse to live by the truth and I will no longer condone and live in your lies. I tried; gave goodness unto all of you and instead of securing goodness unnu du all fi kill it.

<u>No people and family don't just look at me, look at what Good God has and have been doing for us. He's being trying to secure us and we are the ones to refuse him.</u>

We are the ones to accept lies over him; so pay the consequences now because billions of you are going to pay; die. There is no turning back for billions of you because you made it so. SO YOU HAVE NO ONE TO BLAME BUT YOU.

<u>A parent that truly loves do all the secure the future of their child in a good and true way.</u>

No parent that truly loves their child want to see their child hurt. None want to see them die either. Come on now.

Yes my stomach is in knots because I just officially gave up my apartment. I will officially be on my own. Yes my son is confused and talking stupidness but that's okay. He can talk all the nonsense he wants to talk. I told him long ago to go to school or get a job and he did not put forth the effort. I cannot live in slackness anymore. I don't care if my decision does not make any sense to him. I have to secure me and my life. Now they will know just how painful my life is living with them.

Yes my eldest is mad at me for giving up the apartment but I truly can't do anything about this.

The decision has and have been made and I have to live with it. I have to live and I will not try and convince anyone of this.

Yes I am thinking of my mother and the dream I had with her, but I cannot put that on my head. I know I have to go through hard times as of June 1, 2015 but so be it. I can no longer concern myself with some of my children that truly do not listen. Yes it's sad that I had to do this but this was a long time coming. I am sorry I hurt my eldest son but hopefully one day he will learn to forgive me. He truly did not deserve this because he's more than my backbone when I cannot go health wise.

Good God the hurt and pain is coming now but you of yourself know that I had to do this.

You saw my pain and hurt. I had to escape lest I drop down and die. I could not hold on to a sinking ship. Yes I know I had you but the true financial help I needed, I could not get.

Lovey I am bankrupt. I am financially bankrupt, spiritually bankrupt, health wise I am bankrupt. What more was left for me other than death? I want and need to live and it's not right that I have to put so much pressure on you. I cannot continue to drive you insane anymore.

My sanity is important to me.
Your sanity is important to me.

Life; good and true life is important to me all around. Now I am bankrupt; my life is bankrupt and I have to do something about it despite the pain I have caused my children. They are only thinking of them, but what about me? I've provided for them by giving them shelter, a roof over their heads. My children are not children; they are grown so what say them? I've provided them with all I can and could give them. I've taxed me and you and I can no longer do this anymore.

Wow Good God, truly wow.

Oh Lord truly help me because I more than truly need you. I need a great escape and that escape is you.

I need your comfort and more than loving arms around me because the tears come but I have to hold them back. I have to be strong because I know I am going to lose it all real soon.

No, I will not turn to family I can only turn to you, my true friend. I need you to continue to be with me in this storm because I know it is going to be fierce if not deadly for me given my health issues; situation. And if I have failed you in anyway because of this Good God truly forgive me. If you want to go, then truly let it be so. I will continue to journey on without you.

Lovey I need this change.

I need to leave these prison walls.

I can no longer tax my health here.
I can no longer live for death with my children.

I need to break the bond of loneliness and truly be with you by myself. You see the way I complain to you with them about going to school and cleanliness, and to have your children that you've sacrificed so much including your health and sanity for tell you they don't listen to you, why journey any further with them?

Why do all for them?
Why help them?

You've seen the lack of respect. You have so many of these books that outline my hurt and pain; hence I should have nothing else to say.

If I don't find a place by May 31, 2015 at least provide a place and or lead me to a place where I can bathe and brush my teeth. I know my health is going to take a toll because without medicine I will die, but this is a risk I am willing to take.

Yes I know this is my wakeup call also.

As parents we need to take care of our self. We need to do the things that will continue and or preserve our life. We can't all put things into children that have no self respect or care.

We constantly do for our children and our children fail us; do not care so where does that leave us?

Some of us are so stressed out and haggard out like me that if Good God was not with us, we would be dead and gone already.

Yes you want better for your children but if your children don't want better for self what can you do?

I don't know anymore fam, I truly don't know.

Yes I truly have no home or place to go into hence the apartment search is on for me. I have to begin to do for me and soon.

Yes I am listening to Rise Again by Mr. Vegas and I have to let this song carry me through now.

I have to rise up despite the way I feel.
I must rise because we can't stay down forever.

Ah Good God hold me because the time has come for me to move again and seeing my mother driving me through dirty water does not sit well with me.

My thoughts are on this dream because I know dirty water is not good, but she took me through it fast.

Oh Good God this reminds me of the dream I had about the economy. My economic situation is not pretty hence that dream was for me also. When you fall it's not easy to rise. I know this for a fact hence I truly don't know how long I will be without a home.

Yes I am ready Good God but ready to rise and yes to a large degree fall. So if I fall, will you catch me and make me land on both my feet in a good and true way?

Will you be there to hold my hand and say all is going to be okay; well?

Will you cry for me and say, no, this has to stop with her, I cannot let this be anymore, Michelle deserves better?

Will you stop evil in their tracks when they come to devour me?

Yes the tears are here but I can't cry anymore Good God, I truly cannot. I've been through too much and this is the best I can do, hence I leave my distress and duress in your hand and hands. Right now I need you to help me figure out what to do.

I have to figure things out. I just have to Good God.
So please help me quickly so that I can live with you. Yes it's sad that I have to leave my children but what has to be must be.

Ah Lovey I am now listening to FREE YOURSELF by Alborosie. Truly listen to this song and hear what he said.

He said, "you're the only one that can free yourself."

"Love yourself before you love someone else."

Lovey can I have this dance?

Can we dance to this song because I truly need to be free to truly and unconditionally love you?

Lovey I need to run away with you hence I need to be free from the shackles and chains that bound me; keep me from you. I need you beside me so take my hand and let's fly away together where no one can find us.

Oh Lovey, you are my universe and world and I cannot love another god because I truly and more than unconditionally truly love you to the point of insanity sometimes.

We are more than real so truly free me so that we can continually walk in truth and goodness together. You know that my world is not the same without you.

You know I cannot do without you. I am not silent with you so please do not silence me.

Do not walk away from me nor turn your back on me. I truly need to be free with you. Like I said, I cannot love another god because I more than truly love you.

Do not muzzle me Good God because you are my need in my darkest hour and lightest of days.

Lovey the letter was given and I see my children stressing but it cannot be helped. I will not withdraw this letter. Just as you have shown me certain things, I tried my best to show them. You cannot wait until the appointed hour when it's too late to say you are going to do things. It will not work. You will fail.

Lovey, I have to truly love me because I matter to me and you. I have to live for me and you on this day because you more than matter to me. This has been years coming. What my children don't understand is that their disrespect of me is abuse. Any child that disrespect their parent or parents abuse them.

Abuse comes in many forms. Lovey look how yu tek fi mi abuse sometimes.

Look how yu tek society and or humanities abuse.

You too know about abuse hence I cannot fool myself when it comes to you. I have to add you to the mix as well. Your emotions are important as well.

Your life is important also. So yes we have to truly love ourselves and live. I cannot let anyone take my soul and or spirit from me, and I cannot let them take you from me either because I more than need you.

Am I scared right now?

No I am not.

Do I want to end up in the streets homeless?

No, but if that's ordained for me then so be it. What hurts me is to know that my children knew and know of my health and financial woes and added to them in some way. No not all but some. I took the disrespect Good God and I cannot take the disrespect anymore because it's not fair to me.

I've been told by some not all that they will not listen to me and they don't listen to me. So what do I do if my children are set against me; not listening to me?

I can't keep complaining to you about the same thing each and every day. Something had to give and I gave way. I am giving way to what they want come on now. I have to care about me in so many ways.

I have to look and me and say, Michelle I truly love you because you are truly beautiful in more ways than one.

I need to learn to accept me for who I am and that is a beautiful human being that is more than in love with the god of her choosing and that is you. So truly dance with me and let both of us be free always?

Life is given and you game me life – good and true life, so come enjoy it with me in the Cayman Isle and beyond.

Come on Lovey truly lead the way. Let's hold hands and go; fly away together in a good and true way.

Ah My Darling you are more than truly loved always.

Lovey let me create more than goodness of truth for me and you. Shortly I will be free so let our freedom come.

Let us stay free always like I've said.

As I look to you, truly look to me.

Lovey, let no one come to you with nonsense of me. Let no one tell you that I don't truly love you more than unconditionally.

Let no one tell you lies about me.
Know me and be free with me.
Defend me more than I defend you when I need defending.

Crave and yearn to be with me like I crave and yearn to be with you.

Feel the power and truth of me and enjoy.

So smile for me Good God because soon we will see each and we will enjoy the day.

Yes a new day has come and I have to do things for me and not worry about my children because if I do, I will get stressed out. Yes I gave up my apartment and the mood is different with them. All that did not have a job; were too lazy is now scrambling to find jobs. Yes they have no place to go, hence when your parents or parent is treating you right secure your home with them; your parents or parent. Do not cause them (your parent or parents) undue stress and heartache. Do not disrespect them nor let your friends come into your home; their home and disrespect them.

I've been disrespected all around and now it's time for me to go and secure myself. I have to respect me and live so that I can see another day come on now.

<u>*No one should come in and disrespect your mom or dad.*</u> *Absolutely no one because that's your parents and or parent; is your bread and butter because they are the one feeding you, clothing you, providing you with shelter and money come on now.*

I've done enough and I cannot go anymore. Yes this decision is hurting you all of you, so learn and make better life choices. Do not live for death, live for life because your life is important.

If you have someone that truly loves you, hold on to that person and grow in goodness and truth together and or with them. DON'T HURT THE GOOD AND GOODNESS GOOD GOD HAS AND HAVE GIVEN YOU COME ON NOW.

Good God gave you goodness and you mistreat that goodness and or good person. Then you did not want good for you, and don't you dare tell me about the government either. Don't tell me the government this and the government that because we all know no government official have the best interest of society at heart. When the lots of them get into office they make sure they secure their friends and yes some of those friends are bleeping thieves; murderers.

Hence there is no trust around. We all live by lies and I refuse to condemn myself like you; any of you. Yes it's 2015 and I am learning more and more about liars and thieves, and it's sickening and disheartening that we as a society and as human beings live for lies; live to tell lies to satisfy your thieving and lying agenda; yes murderous and greedy ways.

Tell me something, what does it profit you to lie to someone that cares about you?

Is lying a game to some of you?

No, I cannot play your game hence I have to walk away and put a stoppage to all who are lie to me. I have to walk away from them indefinitely because I don't like to be lied to by anyone. When you lie to me you are raping me of my truth and God, and I cannot continue to allow this. Lies hurt, hence I do my best to tell the truth at all times.

Further, going back to book two, I ranted on Rogers Fido and I misinformed you. My son gave up the Rogers Fido number and got a new number from the phone company he joined when his account; which is my account *(because the phone was in my name)* went into arrears with Rogers Fido. So I stand corrected. My readers please forgive me. And yes misinformation is a bitch but it was not intentional. Trust me I will tell you when I do things intentional.

Tell me something Fam, why is it the ones that you think are different, the ones that you feel so comfortable with are the ones to rip your heart to pieces? Do not lie to me because I will eventually find out the truth because Good God will show me you. Don't play head games with anyone's emotions because hurt and pain is a bitch.

Some people cannot take it and when that person go on a rampage and take out their frustration on you in a brutal way you say I am sorry. If you don't want that person let them know. And yes I am one to talk. I drop hints and I fear hurting people's feelings but I can no longer do this. I can't fear hurting you because I am hurting myself and you in the process. So yes I am a wimp when it comes to telling some people how I feel.

Yes this I truly need to get over.

Oh Lord have mercy because I am dreaming more and more about psychics. Why I truly do not know. This morning April 1, 2015 I dreamt I was in this place. This place reminded me of somewhere in Jamaica. I saw this elderly white lady going into this place; old house. Where she went into the house you could not enter you had to go around. So me and my brother went around and down this old pathway. The place looked so broken down people but when we went around it was different. I found out the lady was a psychic. I don't know why my brother and I went into this place because I was saying to myself in the dream, what could she tell me that I don't know already. Getting to the entrance way, I did not want to go in because I did not want anyone to recognize me. At the entrance this black lady was inside with the old psychic lady. The young black lady had long black hair that I think was braided, but don't quote me on the braids. She was short and stout but not too stout and she had two boys. She looked to be in her late twenties and or early thirties and she was dressed in black. I can't remember if she had something red on her but it's neither here nor there right now. I was listening to her talk to the psychic lady but I can't remember what she was telling her. Going inside with my brother, you had people sitting and waiting on gray chairs for this lady. On one side you had all white men in black pants waiting for her. In the center row to the back of the room you had a couple young black boys that I would peg to be teenagers. My brother and I were second in line to see this lady. She was trying to read someone and she said your name is Edward and the man, young white man said no. So she said (I believe she said, but don't quote me) I am getting the name Edward. She was not picking up on any of the white men. She picked up on one of the young black youths and he said that's me. People I know the lady was a fake, could not read people. *So this morning in the kitchen I was talking to Good God; and yes I blasted him because I told him harshly that I am tired of the bullshit and he had better not let anyone tie me again. I told him if anyone tied me again, I would seek to destroy him. I am tired of the hurt and the pain.* <u>**SUH SOEMADY A GUH OBEAH MAN OR OMAN.**</u>

This time around Good God, I will not hold back anything because once this person sey Michelle a guh tie or I am going to hurt her fire and brimstone, hailstorms, thunderstorms nuh fi stop rain dung pan dem. I am tired of the obeah man an oman bullshit. Leave me the bleep alone because I am not bothering you. You as my protector and Good God should more than protect me. Stop letting evil harm your children including me come on now man. I am fed up and tired of it. You as Good God and Allelujah know for a fact without doubt, if I turn from you there is nothing you can or will be able to do to bring me back to you. **Once we are done we are more than done for life more than indefinitely. I am one to carry a grudge and you know this without a shadow of a doubt. If you are my enemy stay that way because I will not make peace with you in anyway. I will walk away from you and find my own. I will leave you alone to your warring and murderous tendencies and ways and wait on time for you to be devoured. I will not and or never lift a finger to hurt you because I have time and know time. I want and need nothing to do with you, so Good God please stop the obeah and false psychic bullshit that's going around.** Yes some people can tell you all about you, but the bullshit lying ones that taint true spirituality; truly shut them down because I am not having it, I am tired of them. No one should make a mockery of the spiritual realm. We are not all spiritual, hence I know the truth of him because you showed me his lies. Hence in due time I must walk away. I will honour my word to him but it is done. It is done, it is done and you know this. I don't like lies. Come to me with the truth and don't lie to me hence there are many dark angels around. Dark angels that kill physically and spiritually. Sex is their drive and aim but it's not mine.

Dark matter and or dark energy exists hence there are dark angels globally.

I don't know people and Fam; I truly don't know why we do things to go to hell?

Look at your life here on earth, some of us are in pain. Now tell me, why would you want to die and go to hell and feel pain worse than what you are feeling right now?

Ah Lovey I truly don't know.
Truly, truly don't know.

Lovey I need you, I truly need you.

Oh ya, wha mek diss man a goa Jamaica?

Lovey, obeah and lodge man business caane stop?

Duppy a guh to duppy.

Male duppy a guh si female duppy. So wait, tell mi sinting mi bunnunoonus, yu a guh mek dem sacrifice someone?

Chicken Gunya wuk, suh happy time come?

No Lovey fi real, di blood letting don't stop inna Jamaica? Suh wait, a seal di casket im a guh seal di casket?

Shi nuh done sacrifice har people dem? Look how many died Lovey? The virus (Chick V) is in the body for 5 – 7 years, now tell me how fair is this to the Jamaica people?

Lovey to me this is another form of AIDS hence I have to watch and see the severity of this germ (Chick V). See what further damage it does to the human body. <u>*Hence the BLACK GUINEA PIGS OF AFRICA AND THE CARIBBEAN.*</u>

Lovey, where is the retribution for the people that died from Chick V?

Tell me something, how can any government use their people as guinea pigs to get a little food to line their own thieving pockets and political agenda of whoredom?

Lovey, like I said, I truly don't want to be any government official globally because many are going to be more than shamed by their children.

<u>2015 IS THE YEAR OF DEATH AND TRUST ME THIS IS JUST THE BEGINNING BECAUSE HUMANITY IS GOING TO FEEL IT HARDER REAL SOON.</u>

Billionaires will become paupers hence the death toll of man will be greater than that of the great depression and all the man made plagues of man combined.

NONE SHOULD CRY AND SAY GOD WHY?

All I have to say to all of you is, look at your sins and tell me where did God come into play? When you were sinning and doing all that is wicked and vile, did you think of him Good God and Allelujah?

So why now that death comes you are thinking of him?

Don't think of him now that death comes come on now.

Lovey, di Kenya trip. Wow. Memba sey, Kenya is that old, and Kenya **HOUSE AND OR HOLD THE SPEAR OF DEATH. SO NOT EVEN DEM OWN CAN MESS AROUND.** So truly good luck with that because **NONE SHOULD COME INTO KENYAN LAND WITH THEIR SACRIFICAL BULLSHIT, HENCE GOOD GOD YOU ARE DULY WARNED.** Remember it was a Kenyan that helped me and I will not let their own sacrifice them unto death. I refuse this, ***so truly tun im back if HE'S GOING TO GO INTO MY LAND OF TRUTH WITH HIS ILLUMINATI, LODGE MAN AND FREE MASON***

BULLSHIT. Africa is not the final sacrifice and or hold of death. Duly remember Mama Africa is tired and I am tired of her deceitful own selling her out to death. Stop death in their tracks now Allelujah come on now. You are the Breath of Life and Mama Africa needs you, she needs your life come on now. I refuse them (these Illuminati, Free Mason, Lodge Man, Obeah Working Satanist) so stand steadfast and sure with Kenya and all Kenyans because the Massai Tribe is a living testament of me and you in some way. (True Heritage and Past)

No more of evil Allelujah come on now. You know the truth of Kenya and how old this land is. You cannot let her own taint her with Satanism, because all is done. Satan lost and you know this, so truly let evil be done now. **You ordained him to do a job and he failed. He did not bring the American debt down, he escalated it. He helped ruin the land and I will not have him ruin Kenya; the mother land in the process.** He joined forces with Satan against you, hence the deed was and is done. America turned from you, hence **YOU MUST NOW TAKE THE EYE IN TRIANGLE FROM THEM BECAUSE HE FAILED.** He failed to secure the future of Americans and you can no longer help and or aide a land that has become worse than Sodom and Gomorrah of their Free Mason book of the dead; their so called holy bible. You and I know that Kenya is an ancient land. Like I said, this land house and have the spear of death that kills Satan; the devil and I will not have him go into Kenya and taint the land. So if you know he is going into Kenya to taint and condemn this land, do not let him go there; shut him out of Kenya. Kenya is important to me because of goodness; kindness and I will do all in goodness and in truth to save them (Kenya) from the devil and the black devils that Satan uses to condemn their own. Like I said, Mama Africa is tired. She is a part of you and you truly have to listen to her. Keep the devil out because he turned from you. He's not a true African so let him be.

It's time now Lovey to set your true people free.
It's time the devil be shut down indefinitely forever ever without end.

No more bloodletting.

Secure your people, and shut di obeah man an oman dem dung. You cannot and or no longer permit wicked and evil people to continue to tie and kill people. Tappi now come on man. It hurts. See my hurt and pain of what she did to me. Tappi man come on now, tappi.

I can't beg you anymore.
I can't plead with you anymore.

Your people including me and my people who is your people are tired. We need to be free. We are trying and you are allowing evil to tie us and shut us down. This is not right nor is it fair. I am fed up of it. I keep telling you true love does not hurt, it's true and you are not listening.

Tell me something, why are you acting like my children and or any child that do not listen? Don't you dare gasp and say HOW DARE YOU?

Don't because you GOT FED UP WITH EVE (EVENING) AND CAST HER ASS OUT. SO WHY THE HELL CAN'T YOU DO IT TO EVIL NOW GLOBALLY? A ONLY YOUR CHILDREN YU HA STRENGTH FA? And no I am not speaking to you as a father this morning, I am speaking to you as my true and real friend. You know I will defend and protect you to the bitter end, so why are you not protecting me and defending me and your people to the bitter end? Black people need to wake up and see their future; end. Lovey hell is full of black people and recruiting more. You know this, so why are you not opening their (black people's) eyes to the truth?

Hell wants them.

You know the truth, so why are you not allowing the Black Race to know the full truth?

Why are you letting evil shut me down?

When you do this, you are telling me that you don't want black people to be saved.

Evil hates you, but I more than truly and unconditionally truly love you. So think and stop allowing death; evil get to me.

As Good God and Allelujah, why are you not casting aside and shutting down all facets of evil; the evil and evils that hurt me and your people? You cannot let evil take final control because evil lost. It's time for all evil to be shut down; so infinitely and indefinitely forever ever without end shut down all evil everywhere.

You want us to praise you, but how can our true and unconditional praise reach you, if all around us is dirty; wicked and evil; sinful; unclean?

Now filth dirty and unclean going to filth dirty and unclean. But then again both lands are condemned anyway. You told me Jamaica is unclean and when death talks about sin, death talk about America, the United States of America. So unclean going to see unclean! Hence Israel and Judah whored and sinned rude and reckless before you; in thy sight.

Ah Lovey you too need to free yourself from the shackles and chains of humanity; humans and spirit. So take my hand and let's walk free together.

Come with me to a pure and better world.
A world of truth.
A world void of all sin and evil.
A world that's for me and you.
Ah Lovey, let freedom be ours forever ever without end.

<u>**Freedom awaits us my dear, so let's take the hand and hands of our people and be free forevermore.**</u>

Come on Lovey let's go.

Let's not wait any longer because the freedom plane has and have come. We truly need to go because Mother Earth is ready, gearing up to give the devil what rightfully belongs to them.

Sufferation, Allelujah, sufferation, Glory to God, sufferation. Let thy will be done Allelujah because it is done. Wow, glory, Allelujah sufferation dey pan lan and many are going to die globally. Lovey, Allelujah and Good God you cannot under any circumstances let your children, lands and people get caught up in this massive sufferation with the devil and their children. If you do you are wrong.

The deed has been done and HUMANS LOST AGAINST THE DEVIL. HUMANITY GLOBALLY CHOSE DEATH OVER LIFE. Humans did not choose life, You, they chose death so because of this, death must take them.

Just as Ethiopia failed.
Eve failed.

The black race failed. Meaning Judah failed. I know not all in Judah failed you, but Judah failed you, because Judah did side with the devil against you. The killings and Obeah activity is there including di bible an key business. **Judah basked in nastiness and now ISRAEL AND JUDAH MUST PAY.** You cannot live in sin and think all will be okay. **EVERYONE HAS AND HAVE FORGOTTEN THAT DEATH IS FOR A TIME AND DEATH IS IN TIME BUT LIFE – GOOD AND TRUE LIFE HATH NO TIME LIMIT. GOOD AND TRUE LIFE IS FOREVER EVER WITHOUT END.**

Good and true life cannot die, but evil and or sinful life dies.

We've also forgotten that the flesh is not life, the spirit is and it's the spirit that feels pain; die and or live depending on your choice in the living; physical world.

We've forgotten that Sin's job was to put enmity between the races globally and Sin has done that. Sin used God – Good God and Allelujah as a mockery, **hence the different religions globally that SELL YOU DEATH AND YOU BUY READILY BUY IT.**

RELIGION DIVIDES AND KILL. SO IF SOMETHING DIVIDES AND KILL, HOW CAN YOU SAY IT IS FROM GOOD GOD?

ALLELUJAH IS THE BREATH OF LIFE, WHY WOULD HE TAKE THIS; HIS BREATH OF LIFE FROM YOU?

WHY WOULD HE GIVE YOU SOMETHING THAT IS SO PRECIOUS AND THEN TURN AROUND AND TAKE IT FROM YOU? Think

because you have a mind of your own. Lovey gave you true life, so live life true come on now.

Death is not a part of Good God portfolio and or Application come on now. You have something good in life and instead of sustaining and maintaining this goodness, you listen to wicked and evil people say death is better. **HOW IS DEATH BETTER?**

No come on tell me, how is death better?

Do you not weep and moan; cry when someone dies? So how is this better? And don't you dare tell me when you die you are going to see your loved ones.

No, I should not be upset at this because billions of you are going to see your loved ones in hell. You're going to burn in hell and die, but not together because some of you are going to spend hundreds of trillions of years burning worse than a bitch in heat in hell. Hence I've told you, I don't want to be no government official that sends people to fight; kill others to keep Aries (Hell) going. Wow, Lord have mercy because your hell hole is deeper than all the black holes of the universe combined. Your hell is so black, dark that the demons of hell need special lighting to see you and inflict more pain on you.

Not even Satan's containment unit is as dark and infinite as yours. When he's dead and gone some of you will still be in hell burning. So truly good luck to billions of you literally because you are going to have hell, no, more than hell to pay real soon.

Death knows me literally hence I worry not about death because death truly knows what I can to. Death can be stopped and Death knows this, but I will no longer interfere with death and what they (death) has to do. **_Like I've said, many lands are going to be destroyed and rightfully so, because IN ALL OF MAN'S GREED, THEY FORGOT THAT HELL NEEDS TO BE PAID; THERE'S A HELL TO PAY AND TRUST ME THEY ARE GOING TO PAY SHORTLY, LITERALLY._**

As humans we don't think. Just like Eve (Evening) did not think and she lost her life we are not thinking and we are losing our lives. Nothing the devil says is true. Say it, *(call me the devil)* so I can blast you. **Lies fuel hell. Our sins keep hell going and they also keep the devil and the demons of hell going; alive.**

Why do you think the devil and his people had to do this?

Sin and or the Devil offered Eve (Evening) all. Did Eve (Evening) get all?

No she did not, so what say you that do the same as Eve (Evening)?

Did you not think you will be punished?

Jesus will save me.

Good keep waiting because like I've said, Good God will never ever send any of his children to save wicked and evil people because you truly do not belong to him. You belong to death. You marry death, sacrifice for death and live for death and die in and for death. You do nothing for life. You do all for death so it's death that must save you. And truly good luck with that because death cannot give life, death can only give death.

Yes Good God's children can stop death because they have the power to. (They are ordained to do so), but they have to be careful because **FEMALE DEATH, NOT MALE DEATH, FEMALE DEATH CAN AND WILL TAKE THEM IF THEY CONTINUE TO PISS HER OFF BY INTERFERING WITH HER.**

These are things the churches do not tell you because they the clergy truly do not know. The devil and his children have to lie to you to keep you coming back. You have your dirty book of sin (your so called holy bible) read it for yourself. This is your nasty truth, **so don't say Good God is going to save you, WHEN YOU LITERALLY GAVE UP LIFE TO ACCEPT BLOOD; THE BLOOD OF MAN BECAUSE SPIRITS HATH NOT BLOOD. YOU ACCEPTED DEATH SO DEATH MUST SAVE YOU. AND LIKE I SAID, TRULY GOOD LUCK WITH THAT.**

Well your mother helps you. My mother is not dead, she's alive and she is with Good God. I've told you in another book, Good and Evil are separated. My mother has her upright eye in triangle. She got her operation already so she cannot die, she must continue with Good God until all who is of God – Good God and Allelujah join them. (And an operation is the best way I can explain it people when it comes to certain changes in the spiritual realm. Good go up to see Good God and Evil go down to see death. Hence the upright and downward triangle of Life and Death).

Know this, Evil sees Good and yearn to be with Good and cannot. Good in the spiritual realm do not see Evil because they are at true peace; rest.

Evil cannot rest, hence they wonder the earth and create havoc on earth and this is due to the amount of sin that is on earth globally.

<u>NO PLACE IS PREPARED FOR THE WICKED AND EVIL BY GOOD GOD. HOWEVER DEATH HAS PREPARED A PLACE FOR THEM AND THAT PLACE IS HELL.</u>

The spirit is energy not blood, so keep your blood and do all for blood. You're all vampires that suck the life out of you and others.

Death is the stay of billions hence man makes diseases, drugs, guns and ammunition, bombs and all that is hurtful, no deadly to kill each other.

<u>This is the life of humanity globally, so now that death comes to take you, you see the tears. LOOK AT YOUR DAMNED WICKEDNESS AND SINS; EVILS. YOU, EACH AND EVERYONE OF US AS HUMANS DID THIS TO SELF.</u>

I did not sin for the next man you are saying. Yes you did, because YOUR SINS AND MY SINS AFFECT OUR ENVIRONMENT, HENCE OUR SINS IMPACT EACH OTHER IN SOME WAY.

<u>*Yes our good impact each other in a positive way but our sins are the deadlier of the two. Meaning it takes a longer time to clean up our sins.*</u>

But, but, but. Stop. The weight of one good is 10 000 and but the weight of one sin is 24000 x2 which is 48000+. I say plus because not all sin weight is the same in my book; plus Death can tack on more time for the weight of one sin. And yes Death has a right to do so because you are in his abode and or environment.

10 000 Ryan and Phillip, no more no less.

But we are physical and spiritual.

Yes we are and the factor does not change for good, it is constant and will always remain constant; the same. And stop with the it's not fair. **<u>Good cannot change; hence GOOD DID NOT PUT YOU IN DEBT YOUR SINS DID.</u>**

The weight of good will never change, hence debts are hard to pay off when you get into it (debt).

Good God can change this you are saying. No he cannot because good life (TRUTH) is eternal, ETERNAL LIFE.

Debts change but Good cannot change. They (debts) accumulate and collect interest, and the longer they (debts) go unpaid is the more interest you pay.

This isn't fair you are saying. And neither are your sins.

God doesn't love us then you are saying. NOPE HE DOES NOT, HE ONLY LOVES YOU SO. Yes so is a great deal, but so is so and not true in my book. So yes God does not love you he only loves you so. (HENCE THE MESSAGE ON THE SCHOOL WALL SAID, FOR GOD SO LOVE US, HE IS WORTHY TO BE PRAISED).

But, but I need his love you are saying. **DO NOT NEED GOD'S LOVE, NEED HIS TRUTH, HIS TRUE LOVE.**

Love hurts and love is hatred and I've told you this. True love is rare; it is true hence it cannot hurt. This is why I tell Good God and Allelujah I don't want or need his loving so, I need his true and unconditional love of truth and true love. When I have this I am more than good to go. I can create a world that is pure and clean, true, good, positive and honest that is void of all facets of sin and evil for me and him, yes including you. Well our good and true people because I truly don't want or need Death's children and people around me. I need true peace and

tranquility and they are not peaceful or truly peaceful nor are the tranquil in any way.

When you truly love someone like I truly love Good God more than unconditionally, all you see is him; them. All you want to do is make life easy and stress free for the both of you; them. As humans we are capable of this, but it's not many of us that want and need this. The offerings and pleasures of the devil are too lucrative and this is why many messengers fail.

I truly don't want or need what the devil has and death knows this. I am more than happy with what Good God has, so why would I want or need another gods come on now?

I don't want or need your idols so don't come to my door with them. When you do I am going to blast my good up good up Gad an im betta shut yu dung. Im betta kip unclean beasts and people from wi door step. Trust me he knows just how nagging I can be. I can nag you to the point of rage and he Good God don't want me to nag him to this point. Hence I tell you, I worry not about wicked and evil people because there is an App for them, and that App is hell. I am not bothering you so keep the hell off my lawn and don't come to my doorstep with your bullshit idols, god and gods. I don't need them hence I don't need death. I have life already and I am not going to give up life for death come on now.

I don't want your stinking god and gods because they are not good up good up life. Go to hell and chuck, I have My Darling already and I am not going to leave him for you. I AM NOT A WHORE THAT RUN FROM THIS PENIS TO THE NEXT. Meaning I refuse to run from this god to that god. Been there done that and I am home; home where I belong, hence I am settled with Lovey (Good and Clean Life) come on now.

So come now My True love and secure a good and true place; land for us; our people.

Darling and True Friend, we have to go home now. We have to leave because disaster looms for many and I truly do not want to see their faces crying for food and saying that you are unfair. Come Mi Love, Mi True Love; let's go because the time has come to go.

<u>My hand is outstretched, take it and let's truly go home.</u>
Cayman awaits, Mama Africa await us; so let's go home in pride; true peace and joy; THE BREATH OF LIFE. Oh Lovey I found the perfect house; home in British Columbia for us. Yes I saw some really gorgeous homes in Quebec but I am not sure if I want to go to Quebec. No, I worry not about the language barrier, but my heart and mind is set on BC, British Columbia.

Lovey, truly thank you for being you because after giving in my rental termination I had to retract it. I had to take it back.

Lovey, I talk a tough talk in certain things and I want and need to leave and I am going to. But I cannot go just yet. I have to extend the time of my departure because seeing and knowing that my children are lost without me gave me a temporary change of heart. <u>I have to give them time to find a place.</u>

Lovey, I truly have to think of my first son and like my second son said, mom you can't just find a place for two and leave out the others. You have to think of everyone and to a certain degree he's right, but to the treatment of my last two, no, I truly do not have to think about them. **<u>Then he hit me with no child asked to come into this world. And he's correct but it does not mean that a parent should sit in disrespect all the days of their life with ungrateful and selfish children.</u>**

Lord my first son, bless him and truly forgive him because I know his anger and there is so much he can do. So because of kindness and goodness towards me, truly forgive him for the wrong treatment today. Do not blemish or soil his record because of this because I more than comprehend and over stand. And no, sin cannot put his outburst on his record because I am wiping it off his record. So death can't say on this day April 1st you did this to your mother. Like I said, I over stand and comprehend his actions. No harm was done. I know he was confused and did not know what to do. He is trying and you have to look at that as well.

He is there for me no matter the pressure on him because he is under pressure. He's the oldest one and when I cannot go he steps up to the plate and be the man and woman of the house. So no, Good God I cannot charge him for sin on this day because I know his hurt and pain. I know the struggles he has so yes, I release him from any sin on this day when it comes to me.

So please give us time to save and find a suitable place. ***They asked for time and I've given them time. As for me, we press forward and carry on to victory. So take my hand because we are going and going together.***

Dear God – Good God and Allelujah April 1, 2015 should be one for the record books when it came to me and my family. Lovey, I withdrew my rental termination letter and instead of continually glorifying you and giving thanks my second child made me regret withdrawing the letter. LOVEY HE CRIED – TALKED TO YOU IN HIS WAY AND HE SAID, "YOU SAID TO WALK IN MY SHOES BY DOING THE THINGS I DID AND HE DID." STRESS HIT HIM LOVEY AND YOU GAVE HIM ANOTHER CHANCE AND

INSTEAD OF CONTINUING ON THE GOOD ROAD, AS SOON AS HE GOT A HEADWAY HE MESSED IT UP WITH HIS BULLSHIT. Lovey a suh wi tan fi real?

No Lovey, you gave him another chance because you've been giving this child chance after chance and he's continually messing up by going back to his nonsense. Walk steadfast and true with you Good God come on now. Hence our ungratefulness when it comes to you.

You've proven to me again that as HUMANS, WE ARE NOT LOYAL NOR ARE WE TRUE TO YOU. YOU GAVE MY CHILDREN ANOTHER CHANCE AND MY SECOND CHILD JUST SLAPPED YOU IN THE FACE WITH INGRATITUDE.

So this morning I am listening to Khago BATTLEFIELD because Lovey we are living on the battlefield of man literally. Truly listen to the song because the youths of today refuse discipline. They want to do their own thing.

Listening is not with some of them.
Ambition has and have ran away from some literally.

Lovey, why do our black children want to live like the lost; dead?

They don't want telling. So if you as a parent and father can't talk to them, then what is left for us to do?

Lovey, I need to go but as my children said, I cannot leave and go live on the streets. Living on the streets is my choice. I am sick, but Good God to get away from children that don't listen I will do whatever it takes. I need to preserve our life.

Like I said, listen to BATTLEFIELD by Khago. Many of these children say THEY NEED STREET CREDS BUT LOVEY, THEY DON'T KNOW THAT WHEN THEY KILL SOMEONE, THE ONLY STREET CREDS THEY ARE GOING TO GET IS HELL. DEATH HAS THEM LOCKED HENCE THEIR SPIRIT IS GOING TO FEEL IT BRUTAL IN HELL.

Like I've said numerous times, **I do not know why anyone would want to die to go to hell.** The dead cries but it's because of the noise around us that makes us can't hear them. And yes some people can hear the dead cry in the living literally.

Good God why can't these kids listen to good counsel and council?

Lovey see the goodness you've done for my son and as soon as he's delivered, he ran back to his folly ground. Lovey you delivered me out of hell literally and I'm to turn from you? Hell no. You are stuck with me because I know goodness. **<u>My sister was here yesterday and she said something to my children that they took to heart but with all this said, dem nuh ha ambition fi self?</u>**

Lovey I could not penetrate what my sister was saying and this morning I still can't, but if you feel offended at what my sister said, have ambition and say, no I will achieve, show you that I am better than this; better than what you think of me. I will not end up dead and I will not become a bum in the streets. My way is not your way hence we are truly different in many ways.

Look at how I try with these books. To date I have not sold 1 copy, but I am still going. Days I want to give up and have given up, but my spirit refuse to let me give up no matter how weak I am on some days.

<u>Yes I learnt something yesterday. I learnt no matter how sick you are, meaning you dying some people don't care.</u> All they think of is self hence I cannot be this way. I have to be true to others. All when mi dey pan mi death bed mi a guh help. Lovey, you know me. Even if it's a email of encouragement that I can send you, I will.

Lovey, people lost dem way yu noa.

Wow.

Good God, a everybody tan suh?

Why is it that when you do good, genuinely do good, people are expecting you to ask for something in return?

<u>There is no cost to my genuinity.</u> Enjoy me and have fun.
I truly care about you, so help yourself and those you truly love. Is that so hard? You need help and Good God has given you help; the help you need, hold on to him because he's there for you. STOP MAKING YOUR LIFE A BATTLEFIELD COME ON NOW.

Look not at what your neighbour have or has, look at what you have. And despite you saying I have nothing, you have something. You may not have it abundantly but you have something. Stop living above your means. If you can't afford a thing you just can't. Do without until you can get it. And truly don't go there because I've done without. I've sacrificed it all not just for my children but for Good God also. Remember I told you, I over love him.

I truly and truthfully love him more than unconditionally to the point where I think I am going to go insane. You may not be able to comprehend this true love and or love of truth, but he Good God and Allelujah does.

Listen, my children can tell you how far they have come plus you've got many of these books that tell you. Hence I cannot comprehend why anyone would join death against Good God and Allelujah. Yes I know the full truth now and I don't want to let go of it come on now.

Yes hurtful things and people I have to get rid of and in doing so, I have to think of the best interest of all. My eldest son is happy, he's smiling again and that's the greatest gift of all to me. I heard him laughing yesterday again and I could not ask for a better gift. He was so stressed and confused and now he's at ease. So yes Good God has blessed me in a great way. His smile and laughter outweighs all my pain and hurt on this day.

Plus yesterday he told me he needed $150.00 to put down the dogs and Fam, I could not do that. I cannot put them down. I told him no, I will not put them down; I would seek a home for them. I can't Fam, I truly can't. I may not like my puppy but putting her down is not an option. I know if I was to go into a shelter I could not take them nor would I be able to take them if I lived in the streets. So no, I have to think of them too. My dogs are a part of my family. And in truth, I cannot give up the true love Queenie has for me. We've come a long way to see them go.

Wow, no.

Oh Lord the dreams are there and I dreamt Howard Stern and I had to put him in his place for downplaying BLACK HERITAGE AND LIFE; TRUTH. So to the White Jews that say, BLACK PEOPLE ARE NOT JEWS. LET ME TELL YOU SOMETHING, **GET BACK AND STEP BACK BECAUSE BLACKS ARE THE ORIGINAL JEWS. DULY REMEMBER YOU DID NOT COME ABOUT ON THE FIRST LEVEL OF LIFE; THE MOUNTAIN OF GOOD GOD. YOU ARE ON THE SECOND LEVEL. BLACKS CAME BEFORE YOU, SO TRULY DON'T GO THERE BECAUSE MANY OF YOU ARE IDENTITY THIEVES.**

You ride off the black man's coat tail and steal our heritage, culture, God, life and way of life, *hence when the new kingdom of Good God and Allelujah is formed* **ABSOLUTELY NO ONE CAN STEAL ANYTHING FROM US. NONE CAN STEAL OUR IDENTITY AND SAY IT IS THERES BECAUSE NONE CAN OR WILL EVER STEAL OUR GOD FROM US EVER AGAIN. NOR WILL ANY OF YOU BE ALLOWED IN INFINITELY AND INDEFINITELY FOREVER EVER WITHOUT END. YOU ARE MORE THAN INFINITELY AND INDEFINITELY FOREVER EVER LOCKED OUT WITHOUT END. Yes the thieving and lying ones that say they are Jews, Jewish but are truly not.**

None can steal our land and culture; way of good and true life ever again. Take your lying asses and go to hell. **The BLACK MAN'S GOD IS NOT THE WHITE MAN'S GOD.** Marcus Garvey and not based on hue; colour of skin.

None of you can come and pollute it (our new world and kingdom; good up good up life), nor can you come and pollute us with your religious bullshit, lies and decrepit god or gods bullshit and whoredom.

So to you FAKE ASS JEWS THAT CLAIM TO BE, REMEMBER REVELATIONS SAID, <u>WOE BE UNTO THE JEWS THAT CALL THEMSELVES JEWS BECAUSE THEY ARE OF THE SYNAGOGUES OF SATAN.</u> I DID NOT ORIGINALLY WRITE THIS, <u>YOUR ILLUMINATI AND OR FREE MASON BOOK OF THE DEAD; DEATH CALLED ALL OF YOU OUT.</u>

Trust me, FOR EVERY WICKEDNESS AND LIES YOU TELL AND SPREAD, THERE'S AN APP FOR THAT AND THAT APP IS HELL.

Most of you hate black people but yet steal the life story and stories of black people and call it your own. Hence the Jesus, sorry Zeus bullshit based on Greek Mythology that you spread and tell and fool fool black people gobble it up and say it's theirs.

NO ONE CAN HAVE NAPPY AS PAPPY HAIR APART FROM THE BLACK MAN, THE BLACK WOMAN AND CHILD.

So truly don't come here with your bullshit because I will put you in your damned place. I don't want your god and gods anymore. I was taught to accept them and I've let them go, so I don't want your god of Isaac or your god of Abraham. Babylon's god and gods I truly don't need hence as we Jamaicans say, BUN BABYLON, FIYA FI UNNU. Hence hell is your home and Satan is your god hence the interlocking triangle. **YOU PUT DEATH ABOVE GOOD GOD AND ALLELUJAH, SO TRULY DON'T TRY ME OR TEST ME.** You all know better. **NO ONE THAT SAY THEY ARE A JEW CAN POSE UP THE INTERLOCKING TRIANGLE COME ON NOW.**

WHEN YOU LOCK AND OR INTERLOCK THE TRIAGLES (UPRIGHT AND DOWNWARD TRIANGLE) YOU ARE TELLING GOOD GOD AND ALLELUJAH THAT YOU ARE MARRIED TO DEATH LITERALLY.

You say you are the true Jews, but yet not one of you know this. You should know. I should not have to tell you this. So tell me now, **WHAT PART OF ANY OF YOU ARE JEW; JEWISH. You're all a bunch of wannabees; frauds that claim to be but are not.** Yes not all so Stern, literally kiss my natural brown ass because I know who I and where I came from do you?

REMEMBER, **TRUE LIFE DID NOT START IN MODERN DAY AND OR THE NOW ISRAEL, TRUE LIFE STARTED IN AFRICA (ETHIOPIA) AND JOINED IN SOUTH SUDAN, SOUTH OF GAN, THE GARDEN OF EDEN.** So really and truly DON'T GO THERE. **Israel house not life, EGYPT DIVERTED LIFE, THE BLUE AND WHITE NILE TO YOUR LAND.** So truly don't WITH ME.

Damn stink. Bouy nuh mek mi cuss out wey nuh lef inna yu. We as Black Jews know who we are.

We know our lineage and heritage.

We know where we are from and we most definitely know where we are going.

We transcend time, because we know and have the key to time, you freaking don't. If you did, you would not sell lies and tell lies on the God you claim to love; say is yours.

YOU WANT THE KEY TO LIFE, BUT YOU CANNOT HAVE IT BECAUSE WE THE BLACK JEWS NOT BASED ON HUE (COLOUR OF SKIN) HAVE IT.

Our law and laws are not governed by the laws of man, hence we, not one of us fall under the law and laws of man. We fall under and are governed by the law and laws of Good God and Allelujah.

Death's law and laws DO NOT APPLY TO US. DEATH'S LAW AND LAWS ONLY APPLY TO DEATH'S CHILDREN

AND IF ANY OF YOU WERE TRUE JEWS YOU WOULD KNOW THIS.

A TRUE JEW KNOW THAT GOOD GOD AND ALLELUJAH HAS AND HAVE MADE PROVISION IN THE GRAVE FOR HIS CHILDREN, AND THIS IS WHY DEATH CANNOT HOLD US DOWN LITERALLY.

WE ARE COVERED AND OR CLAIMED BY GOOD GOD ALREADY, HENCE GOOD GOD AND ALLELUJAH WILL ALWAYS AND FOREVER BE OUR RIGHT AND RIGHTS. EVERY TRUE JEW KNOW THIS.

Dear God – Good God what is this world coming to with the young black youth?

Spring has sprung and my second child got a call that his friend has been shot. Lovey, I know this young man. He's humble and do not cause trouble. He works, always trying to find a better way and he got shot. All he was doing was going to the plaza and someone opened fire on him in the plaza. Lovey wha wrang with demya pickney ya?

How the hell can you open fire on someone that has done you nothing from my understanding?

Hence di youths dem gaane, dem gaane. There is no saving them Good God.

Have mercy man, come on now, when is it going to stop, truly stop with the black youths (based on hue) globally?

Have we not been raped and abused enough to have our children; youths continue the trend by raping the black race of their pride and dignity?

Lovey, mi vex because mi noa di youth. Him a nuh pickney wey walk bout and disrespectful from what I see and know.

No man, di youths wey shot him mi vex, truly vex hence I leave them; the people dem wey shot Walter in your good and cable hands. Help Walter Good God because I truly do not have anything bad to say about him.

Lovey, I know death's children haffi walk, but truly protect the good and innocent. It's not death for death come on now.

Good should not suffer for the bad. There is not damned revenge killings here. It's not death for death or life fi life.

You all frigging complain about society, but yet rape self of the society and land you live in. Unnu mek sense?

Truly protect our own Good God because we need you in all that they do. Yes I am learning more and more, and it's beyond me how humans lie to get what they want and when they are caught in their lies, they make you feel like you are the crazy one. Lovey I am tired of men period because I truly think there is no good one out there. They (men) want, but when they get it, they mistreat and abuse it. And yes this goes for certain women as well.

Lovey, if you truly love a person and they love you, why can't you build a good relationship with that person?

Why can't you grow in goodness together?

Lovey, am I the only one out there that is like this?
Am I the only one that looks to purity of soul and spirit, not just for me but for others?

Lovey, am I crazy; nuts to be this way with you?

Lovey I truly don't know anymore because the more I see and learn is the more I want to run away from society.

People too damn lie.

Selfish and self centered.

Lovey, do we need humans anyway? Don't laugh because mi noa sey yu a ded with laugh.

Lovey, humans bleeping get to me. Dem want goodness and when dem get goodness dem abuse it. So why ask for help; goodness in the first place?

You know what Lovey, if I am the only crazy one that truly loves you more than unconditionally, then let it stay like this. Mek mi tan inna fiwi crazy and insane world because I truly don't know what else I can do or say.

Lovey, a suh humans a get fool, fool?

Ah Lovey death is walking and talking; claiming lives. But Lovey, Kenya though. **147 killed by Muslim or Islamic Militants.** No, I will not get involved with this because **"OLE PEOLE SEY, WEY NUH CONCERN YU LEF IT ALONE."**

All I can tell Kenya is withdraw their troops from Somalia because the war in Somalia does not concern them.

Kenya is Kenya and Somalia is Somalia. They are an Islamic Nation that fights for death and Good God never sent anyone and or told anyone to go and pick up arms against Death's Children. Hence WHAT DO NOT CONCERN YOU LEAVE IT THE HELL ALONE.

Death will massacre you and this is what we are seeing globally today, hence I fear not them. I WILL NOT FEAR THEM, I REFUSE TO. IT'S TIME THE GLOBALLY COMMUNITY START EVICTING THESE BASTARDS OUT OF THEIR LAND AND LANDS AND SEND THEM THE HELL HOME. I TRULY DON'T CARE IF THEY WERE BORN IN YOUR LAND, SEND THEM THE HELL BACK TO HELL BY EVICTING THEIR ASSES AND CLOSING OFF ALL IMMIGRATION CHANNELS TO THEM. COME ON NOW. STOP OPENING THE DOOR TO DEATH, CLOSE OFF DEATH INFINITELY AND INDEFINITELY FOREVER EVER WITHOUT END.

YOU ARE OPENING THE DOORS TO DEATH, SO WHEN DEATH KILL YOUR ASS SAY NOTHING, DO NOT CRY BECAUSE YOU WERE THE ONES TO LET THEM IN.

Death will do anything to get into your land, and once they get in, they take it over and cause you shame and disgrace. Learn from Eve (Evening). She allowed Death in and what did Cain do?

He killed Good (Abel), this according to your so called holy bible; yes Free Mason book of death.

Good and Evil can never coexist and or live peacefully. *Evil will always seek to destroy and kill good. You all know this, but yet do the opposite of what Good God tells you to do and when you are battered and bruised unnu cry out an sey mi sarry, Laade help me because I cannot go anymore; take the pain.* <u>Stay and take your damned punishment, you did not listen in the first place.</u>

CAN A MAN OR WOMAN INCLUDING CHILD HAVE COMPASSION FOR DEATH KNOWING THAT THEY ARE GOING TO DIE AT THE HANDS OF DEATH?

Don't call out to God – Good God and Allelujah for help because <u>every nation globally is at fault.</u> WE KEEP LETTING THE DEVIL IN AND THINK IN THE END WE ARE GOING TO BE OKAY. WE ARE NOT GOING TO BE OKAY.

<u>EVE (EVENING) DID THE SAME SHIT LONG AGO AND SHE DIED. SO WHY ARE WE DOING THE SAME SHIT TODAY?</u>

Why are we letting the devil and his children in and when they do damage; kill our asses we cry and complain and say, life is not fair and or Good God is not fair, he's abandoned us.

HAS GOOD GOD NOT BEEN TRYING TO TELL YOU THAT DEATH KILLS?

<u>DID YOUR ILLUMINATI AND OR FREE MASON BOOK OF DEATH AND OR THE DEAD NOT SPECIFICALLY TELL YOU THERE IS ENMITY BETWEEN GOOD GOD'S SEED AND SATAN'S SEED?</u> Good God did not put enmity between his seed and Satan's seed. There has always been hatred and strife there. Satan and his wicked brood needed a way in and Eve (Evening) gave them one and look at life today? Messed up and jacked up. After Israel the original Israelites (Ethiopians) sided with evil against Good God evil was locked away; out. Hence the separation of lands long before Moses because like I've said, there was a great man in Ethiopia that controlled the elements, hence Moses went into Ethiopia to him. Moses did not separate the Red Sea; it was separated for him by him, this great Ethiopian man. Hence red tongue an han people a nuh pennyapiny. **Meaning**

there's a lot that humans don't know and it's time we stop listening to fool, fool people tell wi bullshit about BLACK PEOPLE'S PAST – HERITAGE AND TRUE LIFE.

Like I said, it's time black people wake up because RIGHT NOW THE DEVIL; BABYLON AND OR ISLAM IS TAKING YOU AND YOUR LAND STRAIGHT TO HELL. I'VE TOLD YOU HELL IS FULL OF BLACK PEOPLE AND RECRUITING MORE.

Good God loves you the black race so much and none of you can see this.

Why are you allowing evil condemn you and your land? Stop the fighting and live. **HENCE KENYA YOU CANNOT RETALIATE AND SAY, YOU ARE GOING TO MAKE WAR WITH SOMALIA BECAUSE YOU ARE WRONG. YOU ARE KILLING THEIR PEOPLE AND WITH DEATH'S PEOPLE IT'S LIFE FOR A LIFE. WITHDRAW YOUR TROOPS AND PEOPLE FROM SOMALIA BECAUSE THE WARS IN SOMALIA CONCERNS YOU NOT. LEAVE THE DEVIL AND HIS CHILDREN ALONE. THEY ARE AN**

ISLAMIC STATE YOU ARE NOT; WELL NOT ALL, SOME KENYANS HAVE AND HAS SIDED WITH THE DEVIL, HENCE THEY SAY THEY ARE MUSLIM. EVERY MUSLIM TAKE FROM THE BREATH OF LIFE SO LEAVE THEM ALONE. THEY SAY ALLAH BUT THEY MASSACRE AND KILL LIFE, HENCE GOOD GOD KNOWS THEM NOT LITERALLY.

You are being warned Kenya, so truly and duly come out of the devil's land because the devil concerns you not. Like I said, you were wrong to interfere. Death cannot be stopped with violence, death can only be stopped with truth, true and clean prayer and all Africans know this but yet you do the alternative and or alternate.

VIOLENCE BEGETS VIOLENCE.
VIOLENCE BEGETS HATRED AND STRIFE.

IF A MAN AND HIS PEOPLE INCLUDING COUNTRY HATES YOU FROM THE

CONCEPTION OF TIME, THEY WILL NEVER LIKE YOU OR TRULY LOVE YOU BECAUSE HATRED AND STRIFE IS ENGRAINED IN THEM.

THE DEVIL'S PEOPLE DO NOT LIKE GOOD GOD'S PEOPLE, SO WHY FIGHT WITH THEM AND FOR THEM?

WHY GO ON THE BATTLEFIELD WITH THEM AND DIE LIKE THEM AND FOR THEM?

<u>Religion is Death's tool against Good God and his people, so why are African's siding with Death against Good God.</u> I've told you Mama Africa is tired, so why the hell are you people giving Death victory over you and your land; Mama Africa?

Africa is not a **RELIGION NOR DID GOOD GOD GIVE ANY OF YOU RELIGIONS OF MEN TO CONDEMN SELF AND LAND BY. YOU CHOOSE TO ACCEPT DEATH JUST LIKE EVE (EVENING) AND NOW LOOK AT AFRICA; BATTERED AND BRUISED.**

Do better for you land come on now.

STOP BEING THE BEATING STICK OF THE GLOBAL POPULATION. HAVE SOME DAMNED AMBITION FOR LAND AND SELF.

GOOD GOD BLESSED YOU WITH ALL ABUNDANTLY AND BECAUSE OF GREED UNNU WANT MORE; NUY WANT WEY IM GI UNNU. WHAT THE HELL MORE CAN HE GOOD GOD AND ALLELUJAH GIVE TO THE LOTS OF YOU? HE GAVE YOU LIFE AND STAYED; JOINED LIFE IN YOU, AND YOU SAY NO. SO STAY BEING BEATENED AND RIDDICULED. DON'T COMPLAIN BECAUSE IT'S A SELFISH AND UNGRATEFUL CHILD THAT DO NOT WANT BETTER; GOOD FOR SELF, FAMILY AND THE LAND THEY LIVE IN.

When you do this (fight for the devil and with the devil), you are hell bound. Your name and your country's name is written in the book of death. YOU VIOLATED DEATH'S CHARTER OF RIGHTS AND WHEN YOU DO THIS, DEATH'S CHILDREN HAS AND HAVE ALL RIGHTS TO KILL YOU IN RETALITATION.

Like I've said above, Good God's people are not governed by the law and laws of death. But this does not mean if you violate death you will not be punished. You will be punished because Death's law specifically said, "THE WAGES OF SIN IS DEATH." So when you sin, take a life, DEATH CAN SWOOP IN AND KILL YOU.

You violated the law and laws of death and death is retaliating by doing his and her job, and that's killing you and or your citizens.

Mama Africa is tired and no one is listening. YOU AS AFRICANS ARE DISGRACING HER (MAMA AFRICA) AND PUTTING HER TO SHAME. You cannot say you are Africans and rape Africa of her pride and dignity; truth and glory come on now.

Right now the devil has won over man. Like I said in another book, these killings are just icing on the cake for death because billions of you have your name and number in the book of death. Come on now man stop this trend. **<u>Instead of trying to retrieve and or take your name out of death's book, you continue to add more time to the number you already have.</u>** Listen, when you are in debt it's hard to come out of it without help. It's the same for your sins. Like I've said, one sin can be 24000+ years. Tally up all your sins that you know of and multiply those sins by 48000 years, then multiply those sins and or each sin total by the amount of years you've done them for, and you will get the amount of time you are going to burn in hell if you have not made amends for those sins. And yes tack on a little extra time because death will. Also know that death don't have to release you from your contract with death, and death won't. Hence death tries to eliminate all who are good. Why 48000 years. We are both physical and spiritual beings hence when you sin in the flesh you sin in the spirit also.

But, but, but. There are no buts. This is every human's reality. You cannot do wrong and or sin and think you are going to get away with it. In all that we do that is wrong; sinful, there's a hell; hence I tell you I leave wicked and evil people alone. There's an App for them and that App is hell. I know what hell's fire looks like and I know what hell looks like. So Kenya come out of Babylon because Somalia is BABYLONIAN LAND. Leave them the hell alone.

Remember, this is the final days of man and many lands are going to be destroyed literally. **<u>If your name and the name of your land is not in the BOOK OF LIFE THEN FORGET IT. YOU ARE GOING TO GO DOWN WITH BABYLON AND BABYLON'S CHILDREN TO HELL.</u>**

Let it go and let wicked and evil people go. You have the spear of death and no one can take this from you. Your land is ancient, so go back to living clean. The sword and or spear of God – Good God is with you, so go back to walking and talking right with him Good God because Death must take their wicked and evil people home.

The Waters of Life must flee from man; wicked and evil lands and people.

Food wicked and evil lands will not have soon because the Earth must turn from them. Hence cannibalism is going to be the norm in many lands. THE MENU WILL LITERALLY SAY, NOW SERVING HUMANS. So Kenya truly let Death and his people go because I am with you and Good God is with you also. Listen. Yes it will be hard but truly listen. Break away from evil come on now. If God – Good God is with you, no one, absolutely no one can stand against you or be against you. You are well blessed and protected come on now.

<u>Two wrongs cannot make a right. You are killing Somali's and you cannot do this because Somalia's war is not Kenya's war. I</u>

do not care if they are Africans and you share a common border. Somalia has and have turned against Good God and Allelujah, hence they massacre life for their god Death. You are of life, continue to be of life and live.

YOU CANNOT HOLD A MAN OR COUNTRY GUILTY WHEN YOU ARE GUILTY ALSO. Come on now.

YOU ARE KILLING SOMALI'S, NOW TELL ME HOW DO YOU EXPECT THEM TO REACT AND OR FEEL?

What you are doing is slackness; wrong come on now. You of a nation would not want someone to come in and kill your people, so why are you doing it to someone else?

Yes injustice isn't right, but guess what, Good God don't business

with Satan's war and strife, so why the hell are you?

Good God don't tell us to go pick up arms against the next man so why are you?

Why are you feeding the demons of hell your life, your country's life and the life of your civilians and or citizens; people?

You are killing them and expecting the people of the world as well as Good God and Allelujah to sympathize with you. Good God will never sympathize with you or anyone that willingly and knowingly take a life. When you kill you are putting yourself in debt. YOU ARE ALSO DISOBEYING THE LAWS OF LIFE. WHEN YOU

DISOBEY AND DISRESPECT THE LAW AND LAWS OF LIFE, GOOD GOD CANNOT PROTECT YOU. HE MUST HAND YOU OVER TO DEATH BECAUSE THE LAW SPECIFICALLY STATES, "THE WAGES OF SIN IS DEATH." You killed so death must kill you. Like I've said, with death, it's death for death and or a life for a life.

Yes eventually death is going to die, but that's hundreds of trillions of years from now. Hence humans have made DEATH INFINITE AND INDEFINITE FOR NOW. TRUTH IS MORE THAN INFINITE AND INDEFINITE BECAUSE TRUTH HATH NO END BUT LIES; SIN HATH AN END and I've told you this in some of my other books.

No one can say they care about Good God and kill; absolutely no one come on now.

LIFE – GOOD AND TRUE LIFE IS GIVEN, BUT AS HUMANS WE CHOOSE TO WALK ON THE CROCKED ROAD AND THINK THAT EVERYTHING IS GOING TO BE OKAY.

Good God is not crocked hence there are no short cuts to him. All good and clean road and roads lead to him. It's just we as humans want things a different way.

It's 6:08 am Good Friday (April 03, 2015) and I've been up for a while. Yes I should be on the beach in Cayman walking but I am not. I have to be content with where I am for now. But soon Cayman I will be there to swim in your sea. Oh man people, wow because I see myself, well my spirit on a massive cyclone. I can see the eye just like the typhoon that's to hit the Philippines. It's like you're on a giant octopus being whipped around in fun; joy if that makes any sense. Weird but typhoon's are beautiful.

Now you are saying, oh my God she's gone crazy. No I've not gone crazy, my spirit is now seeing the water world and it's free. Extremely dangerous and deadly for some but for me calm, truly peaceful; serine. Yes this is the life for me because water can be so calm but yet so deadly.

Hopefully one day I will get into Water with you and how to wrap the bodies of waters around you. Yes it's playful and fun to me and it could be for you too.

Yes I am listening to Total Praise by Fred Hammond this morning. Hence the spirit is calm and relaxed. Have to try and get back to sleep because I need it.

Wow Good God because I truly don't know. My mood is different on this day. It's April 05, 2015 and this is shaping up a bad week for my second child. Last week his friend got shot and now on April 05, his other friend's father dropped down and or collapse in church and died.

Ah Lovey, what to do because death is all around. The day before I dreamt chicken, seasoning whole chicken and cutting off the head of the dead chicken.

Yes I am dreaming about American actors. Dreamt James Franco and I were in bed and he had hair on his back. **Lovey, I can't make any sense of my dream world, All I know is death is all around and many people are going to drop out for 2015.**

I don't know what 2016 holds so truly hold steadfast to your people because evil; wicked and evil; greedy people has and have done the damage, hence death must walk and talk without remorse.

Wow because the tears are here and it's going to get worse. All I ask Good God right now is for you to hold on firm to your good and true people.

It's weird, I saw Shaq and this is what I wrote.

Lovey we need to be in the Cayman Island right now.

I should be looking out at the sea or ocean right now writing to you, but unfortunately I cannot be because I am not financially stable; rich.

Lovey there is so much I want and need to do but I am financially restricted; poor.

One day I know you will lift me up to your glory and I will feed more than multitudes.

We will provide a positive and true environment for our people. But Good God this isn't why I am writing you this morning. Yesterday April 03, 2015 (Good Friday) I saw Shaquille O'Neal's face before me.

His face appeared to me in my waking and or visual state.

Lovey his eyes were closed and it was as if he was dead. You could see his dead stage and or death state.

No light was around him just death. He looked like a dead person; hath no life. Lovey this image stayed for a while so I truly don't know. Don't know what to do or what this mean.

Shaq was dead Good God. These visual states I know nothing about. I cannot put one and one together with these pictures – natural state or waking visions.

Maybe someone is going to die in his family……but I truly do not know because this world is truly different. When I see things that picture is held in my brain; sight for awhile. I cannot shake the image.

So I have to watch this natural sight vision. But Lovey why Shaq? Why did I see him dead so naturally before me?

Is something going to happen to him?

<u>Lovey Shaq is my fun and play and I would hope you would protect him despite the tattoos on his skin.</u>

Michelle Jean

Fam, I truly don't know what to make of my waking state visions. They are so vivid that it is scary at times. It's funny I saw Shaq dead on Good Friday and on Easter Sunday my son's friend father died.

Weird.

Like I said, I cannot comprehend my waking visions and or images; pictures of people that appear before me. Maybe nothing is going to happen to Shaq because I know that death masks death when it comes to me sometimes. It's like death is toying with me to me. But if I was Shaq I would guard my health. Meaning have regular checkups of his internal organs and put down any unhealthy lifestyle he's engaged in if any.

On April 04, 2015 I also wrote this.

Lovey, Good God and Allelujah wow because I don't know what to write.

The eye of the typhoon and the image of Shaq lying there in a dead state still linger in my mind.

Yes I am lying on the typhoon and enjoying because it's a fun ride but to see the image of a dead Shaquille O'Neal scare me. No not scare me, but baffles me because I truly do not know what these images mean and or represent.

No I will not focus on these images because like I said, I truly do not know what they mean.

Maybe Shaq needs to get a thorough check up of his heart and or internal organs; structure.

Wow Lovey this is weird for me.

And no I truly won't bug you about Jamaica because I've been watching more and more Vlogs about there.

The island is truly green and beautiful, but I cannot let the beauty of their fool me because you deemed the island unclean and I have to live with this. Hopefully one day the island can come back clean. Lovey I yearn home but I cannot disobey you. I have to stay focused on what you need me to do.

I know Cayman lack the trees I need but there's nothing I can do about this. This is the land you chose for me and you. Yes I truly don't know why but I cannot question your decision.

Jamaica is hilly, the Cayman is flat.
Jamaica has the Blue Mountain, Cayman does not.

You know what, let me let it go because I truly do not want or need to upset you. True happiness comes for us. It's just unfortunate Jamaica and Jamaicans cannot see their deaths before them due to their wicked and evil ways.

Michelle
April 04, 2015

Fam, my waking visions baffle me because what they represent I truly don't know and it's not like I have anyone to turn to apart from Good God for clarification and that is not forthcoming. So I've learnt to leave these visions alone because they are truly different.

I don't know if this type of death is seeking something and or trying to tell me something by using someone else as a conduit.

Like I said these visions baffle me, so Shaq do not stress about this vision because death maybe using your image as a conduit. But still check out your health and do all to keep healthy.

And please do not ask what American men have to do with me because I truly do not know. All I know is that I am dreaming about them more and more. Dreamt about Morris Chestnut and he was driving me somewhere. Well I was in his car with him. Fam, he took the road to the right of us and you could see the broken road and traffic jam. He could not really move. Pure obstacles in his pathway, so I told him to take the road on the left. The road on the left had a median in the middle to allow two cars to go through. He listened to me and took the road on the left and he just went straight through without any problems. After he went through he turned right. After overcoming his obstacles we were walking hand

and in. Yeah me because people he was not in black. He was in brown; brown suit and this is a plus people because I am so used to seeing men in black; the colour of death; well the physical dead.

Yes there are more dreams but I really can't remember them, I just have to leave them. When they happen I will remember.

Oh man how could I forget this one.
Oh My God, I forgot about Russia.

Dreamt I was in Russia and no, Prokhorov is not involved in this dream. Family this dream is weird because everything was in a rush when it came to me. It's like these men were rushing to give me something to do with food; cheese. **The rush they were rushing everything became dry like dry sticks on a tree.** Yes odd because Russia you cannot rush anything in life. If you want change, change gradually and or slowly. **Do not rush or you will fail; become dry bones like the days of Elijah. And I truly do not want or need to become dry bones with you. I truly do not need the dry Bones of Russia. I need good and true life and this is what I strive for.**

Change must take place, but change does not happen overnight nor is it rushed. You have to know what you are doing and take your time. You cannot be blind to the future; tomorrow. Remember, I did dream that Russian

Men; Business Men are blind when it comes to business. So stop being blind and open your eyes. Also your citizens have to learn to save financially and not spend it all because it's not every land on earth that is going to be destroyed. Live happy but save because there is a future; brighter tomorrow for hundreds of millions.

Yes the future will be bleak for many lands but don't get caught up in the rush for progression.

Do not say I have to rush to get this and that done. You will fail. TAKE YOUR TIME BECAUSE GOOD GOD'S PEOPLE HATH TIME. OUR TIME CANNOT END, SO GO SLOW AND TAKE YOUR TIME.

Yes billions are going to die but you don't have to die with the billions. Do for your people and preserve their future. Prepare for the days when things will become scarce, meaning lands cannot buy your goods and services because of lack of funds. Yes I know sanctions are put on your land but press on because many in the West are going to die for want; food.

Ensure you have plenty of food and water for your people because drought is coming for many lands. Earth must withhold her goodness to wicked and evil lands. She has to hence you will find water receding.

Yes the death of billions is before 2032 but you Russia have time, I know you do, hence make peace with your enemies and leave them the hell alone. Walk away from them and do not create strive with them. Make sure your people are fed and your reserves are up to par; set right so that when hard time comes your people are safe. If God – Good God is with you then truly stay with him. Like I said, I truly don't know why Russia because you're all racist, but I cannot go against Good God, I have to deliver the message he needs humanity to know. There's a message for everyone and it seems Good God is not done with America for some strange reason. **_Yes I've seen their fall but some of Good God's people reside in America and it's time for them to find home; the home he Good God and Allelujah want and need them in._**

So as I close this book truly hold on Russia because somehow Good God has good things on the horizon for you and I truly don't know why, well why you.

Why not France? No, I have to leave France because the South of France belongs to me. Yes I claim it as my own.

Oh people, I've seen my perfect Russian Condo in Moscow. Family, wow, hence I have to go to Russia real soon. I am so blown away by these Russian Condos.

So yes, when I make it I am so going to Russia to buy a condo because the condo life there is so for me.

So to all, despite the world being on panic mode, I have to stay stress free in all that I do. Russia is vast and big and I so want to explore there. Have to explore Mongolia too.

And yes, we can say all we want about the government of Russia but like I said, what don't concern you leave it alone. **EVERY GOVERNMENT OFFICIAL HAS THEIR APP IN HELL FOR THE WRONGS THEY HAVE DONE, AND IF THEY DON'T BEGIN TO CHANGE FOR THE BETTER NOW THEN TRULY TOO BAD FOR THEM.**

I will always tell you love is hate because it's the ones that say they love you that truly hurt you; causes you pain. **You cannot say you have the best interest of your people at heart and then rape them of everything.**

This is not right this is wrong.

You cannot say the children are the future and rob them; your children of their good and true future. When you do this, they will continue to be lawless and without care if that makes any sense.

Listen, if you don't give a child the right tools and information to succeed, that child will never succeed; he or she will fail come on now. Yes someone can come along and give them (that child) the right tools and information, but why wait on that day when you of yourself can do it right now.

Teach right and grow right come on now.

Evil kills, hence evil men and women make law and laws to protect their evil own. But with all this said, evil thinks not of their end, the end of evil. Evil and wicked people forget there's a hell and all the evil and evils they do, they must pay for it when their time on earth comes to an end. So yes worry not about wicked and evil people and lands because hell is smiling up and down at them.

If you want better for self and land, do good because the evil and evils that you do does affect the land you live in.

Do not strive to go to hell, strive to move forward, go up to see Good God. Hey you don't have to listen to me, but listen to good counsel, Good God.

Life isn't about corruption and cheating your land and people out of what rightfully belongs to them.

Life isn't about controlling and murdering your people.

Life isn't about muzzling the truth. The truth must be told so that everyone can save themselves. Hell is real; we are the ones to let others tell us it is not.

If you care about your country, then truly care about it and under no circumstances should you allow anyone to come in and make your land; home unclean. Another government can't tell you how to live if they themselves are not living right. You can't tell them what to do, so why are they telling you what to do? They are not God. Come on now.

No government should put sanctions on anyone and or convince another land to stop selling to any land. In saying this, no government should be pitted against each other. It's not open season for theft; war. EVERY MAN WOMAN AND CHILD HAS A RIGHT TO LIVE ON THIS EARTH. NO, EVIL HAS NO RIGHT TO LIVE ON THIS EARTH SO I STAND CORRECTED. EVIL AND WICKED PEOPLE KILL AND DESTROY, HENCE I KNOW THEM NOT. Meaning I want nothing to do with them. Hence I will forever ever without end advocate for the Good God and Allelujah, the Earth and Universe to evict them all (all who are wicked and evil). There's no place on Earth for Death's children so they truly have to go by any means necessary. Meaning however Death chooses to walk away with them and or take them is Death's business.

Strife can be avoided, but then the warmongers that feed the belly of Aries the God of War refuse to truly make peace. They would rather fuel their blind ego rather than see the greater good of their people and home; land.

All are so ignorant that they cannot see that they've plunged their people and land to the depths of hell. So no, no government official care about their land and people because they're *selfish and stupid, ignorant and lack truth; goodness and honesty.*

You willingly invade another man's country and kill their people and some of you have the gaul to say, you are going to see Good God and Allelujah.

You're killing your people.
You're sentenced them to hell including the land you live in come on now. So truly don't tell me you care.

Look at how much money the lots of you spend on MURDER; DEATH.

You see the needs and wants of your people and many of you let them (your people) go homeless.

Some are battling diseases that you created.

Some are frigging insane because of the food and drugs you give them to take another human beings life.

Some are so deranged that they commit suicide. So no, I truly don't want to be any of you in the grave or on earth right now because YOU'VE ALL BEEN SENTENCED TO HELL LITERALLY. Yes death and this is your own doing. Do not lie to people. **SACRIFICE IS DEATH. YOU ARE KILLING YOUR OWN TO KEEP YOUR SPACE AND PLACE WITH THE DEVIL COME ON NOW.**

Know this; no one can keep their place with death if they are sinful. Death is automatic. It may not be today, but remember, there will always be a tomorrow. Hence death will always come once you've sinned. No one can escape this judgment. No, the Jews can because the true Jews have a saving grace but billions of you truly do not. And yes I know what I've told you in my other books but keep this new knowledge.

Trust me the demons of hell are waiting with a smile on their faces because if you haven't cried in the living, truly wait until the spirit leaves its jailhouse which is your flesh.

And yes there will be a book four because for some strange reason this book, (book 3) is incomplete to me.

Michelle and Michelle Jean

OTHER BOOKS BY MICHELLE JEAN

Blackman Redemption – The Fall of Michelle Jean
Blackman Redemption – After the Fall Apology
Blackman Redemption – World Cry – Christine Lewis
Blackman Redemption
Blackman Redemption – The Rise and Fall of Jamaica
Blackman Redemption – The War of Israel
Blackman Redemption – The Way I Speak to God
Blackman Redemption – A Little Talk With Man
Blackman Redemption – The Den of Thieves
Blackman Redemption – The Death of Jamaica
Blackman Redemption – Happy Mother's Day
Blackman Redemption – The Death of Faith
Blackman Redemption – The War of Religion
Blackman Redemption – The Death of Russia
Blackman Redemption – The Truth
Blackman Redemption – Spiritual War
Blackman Redemption – The Youths
Blackman Redemption – Black Man Where Is Your God?

The New Book of Life
The New Book of Life – A Cry For The Children
The New Book of Life – Judgement
The New Book of Life – Love Bound
The New Book of Life – Me
The New Book of Life – Life

Just One of Those Days
Book Two – Just One of Those Days
Just One of Those Days – Book Three The Way I Feel
Just One of Those Days – Book Four

The Days I Am Weak
Crazy Thoughts – My Book of Sin

MY TALK – BOOK THREE THE RISE OF MICHELLE JEAN

Broken
Ode to Mr. Dean Fraser

A Little Little Talk
A Little Little Talk – Book Two

Prayers
My Collective
A Little Talk/A Time For Fun and Play
Simple Poems
Behind The Scars
Songs of Praise And Love

Love Bound
Love Bound – Book Two

Dedication Unto My Kids
More Talk
Saving America From A Woman's Perspective
My Collective the Other Side of Me
My Collective the Dark Side of Me
A Blessed Day
Lose To Win
My Doubtful Days – Book One

My Little Talk With God
My Little Talk With God – Book Two

A Different Mood and World – Thinking

My Nagging Day
My Nagging Day – Book Two
Friday September 13, 2013
My True Love
It Would Be You

MY TALK – BOOK THREE THE RISE OF MICHELLE JEAN

My Day

A Little Advice – Talk
1313, 2032, 2132 – The End of Man
Tata

MICHELLE'S BOOK BLOG – BOOKS 1 – 20

My Problem Day
A Better Way
Stay – Adultery and the Weight of Sin – Cleanliness Message

Let's Talk
Lonely Days – Foundation
A Little Talk With Jamaica – As Long As I Live
Instructions For Death
My Lonely Thoughts
My Lonely Thoughts – Book Two
My Morning Talks – Prayers With God
What A Mess
My Little Book
A Little Word With You
My First Trip of 2015
Black Mother – Mama Africa
Islamic Thought
My California Trip January 2015
My True Devotion by Michelle – Michelle Jean
My Many Questions To God
My Talk
My Talk Book Two